GEORGE & ROBERT STEPHENSON

Railway Pioneers

Chris Morris

Ben

Best wishes

— Chris.

AUTHOR'S NOTE

This is primarily a photographic book celebrating the legacy of George and Robert Stephenson; the main portfolio begins on page 23. To set the scene and provide background information, the book begins with a concise illustrated biography of father and son.

Grid references are provided only for the most remote locations.

First published 2010 by Tanners Yard Press
Tanners Yard Press Church Road Longhope GL17 0LA
www.tannersyardpress.co.uk

Text and images © Chris Morris 2010

British Library Cataloguing in Publication Data
A catalogue record for this book is available from the British Library

ISBN 978-0-9564358-0-4

Designed by Paul Manning
Printed and bound in Poland by Polskabook UK Ltd

Previous page: Puffing Billy *(Stephenson Museum, North Shields)*

Contents

"I will do something in time which will
astonish the whole world."

George Stephenson

Steam Power: Foreword by Mark Whitby   4

The Railway Pioneers   7

PHOTOGRAPHING THE LEGACY

Early Days   23

Liverpool to Manchester   39

Consolidation   57

Robert Stephenson, Complete Engineer   83

A Place in History   106

Index   110

Acknowledgements and Further Reading   112

Steam Power

'The patent system added the fuel of interest to the fire of genius.' *

Facing page, left: Richard Trevithick's 1797 model, built to prove the concept of steam locomotion (Science Museum, London).

Right: Mark Whitby in the Institution of Civil Engineers president's office, with a lithograph showing Robert Stephenson's Britannia Bridge.

The story of the Stephensons is about the development of the railways, and the steam engines that powered them. The coming of the railways was not just another technological advance: it encompassed a seismic shift in civilisation from the carbon-neutral agricultural society of the eighteenth century to the carbon-hungry industrial world of today. The steam engine drove the economic boom that literally shook the world: a sense of unease amongst a section of the intelligentsia meant that for some the green and pleasant land turned into one featuring dark satanic mills, spawning a romantic movement that denigrated the artisans of the industrial revolution. But a measure of the lasting achievement of these 'industrial revolutionaries' would be the power that their steam machines ultimately achieved: in twentieth-century America, stationary engines generating electricity for the New York subway were capable of producing 10,000 horse power, while on the railroads, more agile steam locomotives were able to haul loads of nearly 20,000 tonnes.

With a resonance we can feel today, the beginnings of steam power date back to a fuel crisis in the early 1700s; the iron industry depended on charcoal produced from wood, supplies of which became exhausted, or reserved for the use of the navy. A better alternative was found to be coke, derived from coal: mining coal, whilst initially easy, soon demanded deeper pits with a serious risk of flooding. This was tackled at the end of the seventeenth century by Thomas Savery with his invention of the atmospheric steam pump, whose power was derived from the vacuum caused by the condensing of low-pressure steam. Thomas Newcomen worked with Savery's ideas to produce his beam engine, which in turn was elaborated on by James Watt with a separate condenser, doubling its efficiency. Savery, Newcomen and Watt had patented their ideas; this meant that the inventors could each make ongoing financial gain from their work and at the same time force the next generation into creative lateral thinking, getting round the restrictions with ever-improving technology.

At the end of the eighteenth century, Richard Trevithick developed a new lightweight engine whose pistons were powered directly with the expansion of high-pressure steam. Further, he introduced the concept that an engine could drive

* Abraham Lincoln, 1859

its own wheels, a point he ably demonstrated with a steam carriage in the streets of Camborne in Cornwall in 1801. While his principles were vital, he didn't follow through to solve the problems he encountered.

Mechanics on Tyneside carried on Trevithick's work, developing track strong enough to take the weight of the heavy locomotives. George Stephenson was not alone in making the concept a working reality, but it was he and his son Robert who developed the railways as we see them today. That George's origins were so humble and his achievements so great is not lost on modern engineers. Today, very few would associate themselves with the negative image the romantics painted of industrial progress, and the artisan mechanics who drove it forward, rather embracing whole-heartedly the concept of the Victorian 'heroic engineers'. Chris Morris clearly belongs to the latter camp and his photographic book gives a visual power to the lives and legacy of the Stephensons.

Mark Whitby
Former president, the Institution of Civil Engineers

The Railway Pioneers

The concept of railways, or of wagons running on a track, dates back to the seventeenth century. These 'wagonways' were in use for transporting coal out of mines; the 'rails' were wooden, as were the wheels, and they were sometimes called 'tramways', probably from the German word 'Traam', meaning 'wooden beam'. By the late eighteenth century, the wooden rails were being replaced with cast iron, frequently of 'L' shape section; these 'plateways' enabled wagons ('trams' or 'drams') to stay on the line without the need for flanged wheels. Up to this point the motive power for the wagons had been children pushing, or sometimes a horse pulling, a 'train' of them. The development of railways as we know them depended on invention and improvement in both the track and the motive power: of these two, the revolutionary aspect was the power.

Cornishman Timothy Newcomen invented the steam engine, first used in 1712 as a mine pump; James Watt improved and developed it into a reliable power source. By the end of the eighteenth century, industry no longer needed to be sited close to water. Huge beam engines, running in their own engine houses, featured in the mining pit-head landscape, and were used for pumping water from the working levels (which could now be much deeper) and for hauling men and materials up and down the shaft. These stationary engines were also used for hauling trains of wagons out of the pit, and onwards to river or canal transport. Still, the main motive power remained the horse.

Before the end of the century, another inventive Cornishman, Richard Trevithick, had developed Watt's huge and cumbersome engine, increasing its power by utilising steam at a higher pressure, while also reducing its size. He then came up with the notion that an engine, instead of hauling its load by a cable, could become a mobile power unit by driving its own wheels, pulling wagons coupled to it. The idea was scoffed at by the establishment, but in 1802, Trevithick had a prototype 'travelling engine' made in Coalbrookdale; two years later, he proved his idea workable, famously winning a wager on a South Wales tramway that his engine could pull ten tons of coal the ten miles from Pen-y-Darren to Abercynon Wharf.

For a decade, Trevithick's ideas were toyed with in collieries on Tyneside and elsewhere, and the development of both engine and track ran in parallel. One of the difficulties perceived by potential investors (mine owners) and trumpeted by the detractors (canal operators and landowners) was the concept of adhesion – the ability of smooth wheels to grip on a smooth rail. One red herring was introducing a 'rack and pinion' drive (of the type used on mountain railways), but it was realised that if the locomotive was heavy enough, there would be sufficient grip without that complication. However, the weight of a locomotive caused other problems, tearing up the old wooden tramways and cracking the cast iron plateways. After years of trial and error, the old rails gave way to more

Facing page: Replica of Richard Trevithick's 1802 prototype for the Pen-y-Darren engine (Blists Hill, Ironbridge Gorge Museums).

Above: Plateway (Blists Hill).

Right: Replica of of William Hedley's Puffing Billy *(Pockerley Waggonway, Beamish Museum, Co. Durham).*

resilient wrought iron track, with no need for a guiding upright, as locomotives and wagons used flanged wheels.

All this developmental work took place in the coal mines, and on their tramway routes to canal or river transport, where several inventive mechanics were experimenting with 'travelling engines' on level sections. The most famous locomotive of this post-Trevithick but essentially pre-railway era was *Puffing Billy*, developed by William Hedley for use on the Wylam colliery tramway on Tyneside. Meanwhile, at the Killingworth colliery to the north, another 'enginewright', George Stephenson, had in 1814 developed his own locomotive, *Blücher*. Stephenson did not invent the steam engine or the steam locomotive, but he was to play the most significant role in the coming railway revolution.

George Stephenson was born in 1781, in the Tyneside colliery village of Wylam. From a young age he and his brothers worked in the mines alongside their father, though they were all in the privileged position of caring for the pumps and other machinery. There was no question of any schooling, but George in particular seemed to have an instinctive feeling for mechanical arrangements. This was matched by both enterprise and stoicism: even before starting at pit work, he filled his time working on a farm, and, as a teenager, ran a business making and repairing shoes. As a maintenance man on the pumps and engines, Stephenson's remarkable early aptitude for mechanical things had slowly won the respect of his employers at Killingworth, who valued his skills and allowed him free rein. By 1813, he had developed a locomotive for the mine.

Keen to do the best for his son, Stephenson senior sent Robert first to the village school at Long Benton and, when he was twelve, to a private school in Newcastle – Dr Bruce's Academy in Percy Street. Thrust into a middle-class society, Robert's education included enrolling in the city's Literary and Philosophical Society. George had reached adulthood illiterate and, determined to improve himself, had been attending night school. He was, in a sense, growing up with his son, who would bring home books borrowed from the 'Lit & Phil' to discuss with his father. Meanwhile Robert was gaining insights into his father's intuitive understanding of practical mechanics.

An example of George Stephenson's instinctive approach to problem-solving was his development of a miner's safety lamp. Responding to a competition, he succeeded by empirical method, risking his life testing his ideas in the mine. Meanwhile in London, the eminent scientist Sir Humphry Davy had solved the problem by scientific principle and, disparaging Stephenson's efforts, was awarded the prize. Thus began Stephenson's lifelong distrust of both academics and southerners.

On leaving school, Robert was sent to Killingworth Colliery to work with his father's old boss, Nicholas Wood. Before the end of his three-year apprenticeship, his father was enmeshed in the planning of the Stockton & Darlington railway, and Robert was summoned to help on the survey. Still looking for the best for him, in 1822 his father sent him to Edinburgh University for a term. Not long, it might seem, but enough to broaden his outlook. Returning, he was thrust right into the front line of the technological revolution. Aged only 20, he was made managing partner of what was essentially his father's new business dedicated to building locomotives, Robert Stephenson & Company.

That might have been the end of Robert's growing up, a rapid rise to the responsibilities of adulthood and total enmeshment in his father's growing business dealings. However, in a completely unexpected and never explained move, he agreed to take a party of Cornish miners to South America to open up and run a silver mine. In some ways it was like a modern school-leaver's 'gap year' before university; but this was no dilettante's grand tour – it was a harsh three-year stint in the wilderness beyond Bogota in the Andes. Did he do it from a sense of adventure, to prove his character, to make his fortune, to take a break from his father's cloying attachment? No one knows, but the latter seems at least part of his thinking. When he returned, he was to be a stronger and more independent force in the burgeoning Stephenson empire.

THE STOCKTON & DARLINGTON RAILWAY

Conceived as a mineral route to carry coal from the mines of West Aukland to the navigable River Tees at Stockton, the Stockton & Darlington railway grew out of several decades of conjecture and inaction. Initially, it was to be a canal, but in 1812, Darlington businessman Edward Pease revived the project as a railway. After rejections and the involvement of several engineers, the line was granted parliamentary approval in 1821. The very same day, Stephenson arrived at Pease's house to offer his services to the project.

Pease was much taken with Stephenson and, putting aside his previous surveyors, offered him the chance to develop the railway. This was to prove a pivotal moment, and one antici-pated by the visionary Pease: '… to convey not only goods but passengers, we shall have the whole of Yorkshire and next the whole of the United Kingdom following with railways.'

Steam locomotion was not part of the plan: no-one, apart from Stephenson, could visualise 'travelling engines' working away from the pit tramways. The new survey was for a line to be worked in part by horses and by fixed engines, with rope haulage on its inclines. As the line progressed, built to Stephenson's preferred gauge of four foot eight and a half inches (by repute the width of a wheeled axle since the days of the Romans), Pease was persuaded to use the newly developed wrought iron track, although it was twice as expensive as cast iron. For horse-drawn trains this would not be vital, but it suggests Stephenson was looking ahead to steam locomotion – it certainly was not a recommendation in his short-term financial interests, as he was still in a partnership producing cast iron rail.

Next, Pease was invited to Killingworth to see the latest development of Stephenson's engines at work. He was very impressed: by the time of the completion of the line he had swung his committee behind steam locomotive power (though the line still included inclined planes with rope haulage, and horses pulled passenger trains until well into the 1830s).

For the railway's 1825 opening, the new and further refined locomotives Stephenson had supplied from his recently estab-lished works in Newcastle included the famous *Locomotion*. Until the coming of the Liverpool & Manchester five years later, this line was to wave the flag for railway innovation.

Right: Locomotion, *detail (Head of Steam Railway Centre and Museum, Darlington).*

Far right: George Stephenson's Stockton & Darlington travel pass (Chesterfield Museum).

THE LIVERPOOL & MANCHESTER RAILWAY

In the final years of the eighteenth century, as both Liverpool and Manchester grew at an exponential rate, a resentment festered about the monopoly of trade between the two cities enjoyed by the Bridgewater Canal and the Mersey/Irwell Navigation companies. Surveys for a horse-drawn tramway by William Jessop and Benjamin Outram in 1797 and 1798 led to nothing for lack of financial support. In 1821, William James, an influential and outspoken advocate of the railways, arrived in Liverpool and was successful in gaining backers for the same scheme. A meeting with George Stephenson rapidly won him over to the benefits of steam locomotive power and the same year, he became a partner in Stephenson's business. In 1822, the Liverpool committee formed to promote a railway gave James the go-ahead to organise a survey; the team of young surveyors included James's own son and the young Robert Stephenson.

Surveying the line was not easy: as well as physical difficulties – crossing the bog at Chat Moss, the wide Sankey Valley and a deep rock cut at Olive Mount on the eastern edge of Liverpool – the widespread opposition from vested interests led to violent intimidation. Despite this, the survey was completed rapidly, but William James, having over-extended himself on other projects, dragged his feet. In 1824, the committee sacked him and appointed George Stephenson as engineer. Stephenson was also a busy man and, while appearing to make rapid progress with a final survey, was in fact not taking enough care. Before parliament in 1825, the opposition lawyer tore Stephenson to shreds, mainly over the levels (which any engineer – including Stephenson himself retrospectively – would agree were at fault), and the bill was inevitably lost.

Above: Medallion, Sankey Viaduct (Chesterfield Museum).

Left: Liverpool & Manchester carriage (National Railway Museum, York).

Below left: Tunnel vent at Crown Street, site of Liverpool's original terminus.

Above: Sankey Viaduct, Newton-le-Willows.

engineer, but Vignoles appeared to be shabbily treated, being relegated to the role of assistant to Stephenson, who rapidly found an excuse to sack him.

With all these dramas out of the way, George Stephenson could get on with the practical problems of building the railway. Construction was well in hand when the company found itself running short of funds, a horribly normal circumstance on this kind of project. The ensuing application to Westminster for an additional exchequer loan met with the equally normal response: the Loan Bill Commissioners, whose chief engineer was the eminent Thomas Telford, would have to inspect progress on the line. In late 1828, Telford himself made a trip north. Well known for his principle of separating specifier from contractor, Telford disapproved of Stephenson's day-by-day involvement in the construction (he was said to even be supplying the wheelbarrows). While he found a lot to admire in the progress of the line, Telford judged the survey and plans inadequate and the management un-businesslike, forcing the company and their engineer to rewrite their contracts before receiving their loan.

Telford's other concern was what motive power the line would use, for it still had not been decided. Amongst the promoters there was serious disenchantment with the concept of 'travelling engines'; despite the success at Stockton, they believed fixed engines and haulage would be needed, not just on the inclines, but along the whole route. The case against locomotives was that they were dirty, noisy, underpowered and unreliable. In what may have been the last chance for the locomotive lobby, a challenge was set up on a completed section of track at Rainhill to test, not just one engine against another, but the whole concept of steam locomotion.

With the opening of the Stockton railway, Stephenson's ego very quickly recovered. Remarkably, the Liverpool committee were forgiving, retaining faith in their engineer's practical abilities, but deciding to get a smooth talker in for their next attempt at parliament. In May 1826, the railway was granted parliamentary approval thanks to a modified survey and presentation by Charles Vignoles, supervised by the Rennie brothers. But putting the plans into practice was like a game of musical chairs: the various engineers invited to work in tandem were too proud to share the job, and walked out. The process ended up rather luckily for George Stephenson, with his recall as chief

ROCKET AT RAINHILL

Although he had helped on the survey of 1823, Robert Stephenson was away in South America during all the subsequent turmoil of getting the Liverpool line underway. In his absence locomotive design had languished, but he had been back a year, when, in the spring of 1829 the Rainhill trial was announced to take place in October. Understanding the significance of the trial, he and his team designed a new engine, *Rocket*, specially for the event. Two new features were to give *Rocket* an edge: a set of steam tubes in the boiler, giving vastly improved water heating, and the setting of the cylinders outside the boiler and at an angle of forty-five degrees (later altered to be almost horizontal).

Of the five entries, two were rapidly discounted as they did not even start – the ultimate reliability failure. Alongside the Stephensons' *Rocket* was *Novelty*, from the London firm of Braithwaite and Ericsson, and *Sans Pareil* from Timothy Hackworth, who had worked with Hedley on the *Puffing Billy* and was in charge of the Stockton & Darlington yard at Shildon. The press favoured *Novelty*, with its pretty appearance, all covered in copper like a fancy parlour kettle. Technicalities aside, it is sufficient to say that *Novelty*, after a promising start blew up, and that *Sans Pareil* ran reasonably but with increasing difficulty on successive runs, exhibiting a serious safety disadvantage by blowing red hot cinders out of her chimney. *Rocket* behaved impeccably, and further along the line went beyond the call of duty, unflaggingly pulling its load up an incline.

Rocket did more than win the £250 prize at Rainhill. It set new standards for reliability and smooth running and established beyond doubt the viability of steam locomotion. From now on, objectors would be onlookers to what would soon be a universal rush to embrace public railways and the revolutionary concept of the 'travelling engine'.

On 15th September 1830, a year after Rainhill, the Liverpool & Manchester railway staged a grand opening. The huge crowd included a long list of VIPs, headed by the Duke of Wellington, and the company ran no fewer than eight trains on the double-track line. In earlier test runs, unprecedented speeds of 35 mph had been recorded, but there would be no such risk-taking on this gala day. Sadly, the event would be remembered for a fatal accident: during a lull in proceedings, VIPs left their stationary carriage for an innocent stroll on the line, and Westminster MP William Huskisson was knocked down by a passing train. The accident marred the proceedings but could not mask the engineering success of George Stephenson's big day. By 1830, the railway revolution had been won and all that followed would be consolidation.

Left: Rocket, *detail (Science Museum).*

Right: The bridge over Rochdale Canal at Gauxholme, Todmorden.

CONSOLIDATION

The Liverpool & Manchester was the first line planned to take passengers and to rely on steam locomotion, and it rightly takes pride of place, along with *Rocket*, in railway history. After the opening, George Stephenson was flooded with propositions for new lines and he accepted almost all, without much regard to how he would manage them.

Amongst all the adulation came a setback. One of the new projects was the Grand Junction, an important route which was to connect Birmingham to the Liverpool & Manchester line. Stephenson sent his star assistant, Joseph Locke, to make a survey and in 1833 his route was approved in parliament. Locke, naturally, hoped he would be made engineer, and the board would have favoured that, but the omnipotent Stephenson made it clear that that should be his, Stephenson's, role. Locke was tired of playing second fiddle while others took the credit for his work, and threatened to walk out. The board reached a compromise: Stephenson would be in charge of the southern half of the route and Locke the northern. How unhappy Stephenson was with this is not clear. Perhaps he took his eye off the ball, for certainly his bad old habit of sloppy surveying and estimating, in contrast to Locke's clarity and precision, led to delays and bad feeling, and it was Stephenson who resigned.

The resulting rift between old master and pupil was never bridged.

Many of the new proposals were for passenger lines, which would in time form the basis of a national network. By the mid-1830s, Stephenson railways ran, or were planned, to Derby, Leeds, York and Sheffield. On the other hand, the proposed route from Leicester to Swannington was purely an old-fashioned mineral line, aiming to serve an area of coal mining with poor transport links. Insignificant though it seems, taking it on reaped an unexpected bonus for the Stephensons. During cutting for the line, Robert discovered hitherto untapped coal seams. Sharp as a spade, his father dug up a couple of Liverpool cronies as partners and bought a big estate, opening up the Snibston Colliery. The seriousness of the old man's intention is underlined by the family moving from Liverpool to Alton Grange, near Coalville. The former colliery worker had now become a landowner and country squire.

Increasingly acting independently of his father, Robert suffered a setback of his own. In 1832, while acting as advisor on the Stanhope & Tyne, a proposed mineral line in County Durham, he agreed to accept his fee in company shares and failed to notice that the company was not limited. A combination of reckless payments for land rights, erosion of viability of the line by rival routes and general mismanagement led the company into serious financial difficulties. All other substantial investors pulled out, leaving Stephenson facing ruin. He was saved by his father's friendship with George Hudson (of whom more later), who, by various manipulations of companies in which he had an interest, incorporated part of the Stanhope line into the first through-route north. This added to its value, luckily enabling young Stephenson to extract himself without major losses.

THE LONDON & BIRMINGHAM RAILWAY

With their interests spreading all over the country and into Europe, in 1836 the Stephensons opened an office in London. Three years earlier, Robert had moved south with his wife Fanny to live in Haverstock Hill. He had been named engineer to the London & Birmingham railway, a project dwarfing earlier schemes. With this appointment, it seems the son finally broke free of his father's controlling presence. There had never been animosity between them, but, despite his obvious talent, the son had always been in the father's shadow.

This new project was four times longer than the Liverpool to Manchester line, and there was no talk of needing rope-hauled inclines, though this meant many long cuttings and tunnels, some through unexpectedly difficult geology. Despite formidable opposition from landowners and from the vested interests of the turnpike and canal operators, the bill went through parliament first time, smoothed in some instances by

Below left: Kilsby, tunnel vent.

Below: Hownes Gill, Stanhope & Tyne.

Right: Winkwell Bridge. The original cast iron ribs are now cased in concrete.

Far right: Reflection of Wolverton viaduct on the River Ouse.

Facing page: Snibston Colliery Museum, Coalville.

paying inflated land prices to the petitioners. Stephenson approached the management of the building of the line with the respect it deserved, splitting it into sections under resident engineers and taking overall rather than intimate control. The sections were subdivided into contracts of usually only six-mile lengths so as to not overstretch the small contracting companies – the days of huge contractors with armies of navvies were yet to arrive.

Keeping the gradients manageable for the locomotives of the day was an immense engineering task, involving tunnels, embankments and cuttings on a scale reminiscent of Thomas Telford's last canal, the Birmingham & Liverpool – itself built straight and level like a prototype railway. One of the obstacles was the range of the Chiltern Hills at Tring. Even more difficult was Blisworth near Northampton, where the cutting was through broken rock and soil saturated with springs, and the tunnel at Kilsby, where the line ran through quicksands. All these obstacles had to be overcome by men with picks, shovels and wheelbarrows. An extension of the line from the original terminus at Chalk Farm into the centre of London at Euston could not comply with Stephenson's strictures on gradients, and initially a fixed engine had to be used. The line was opened in 1840, beating Brunel's Great Western into the capital by a year.

By the late 1830s, with his son triumphant as engineer of the London & Birmingham, George Stephenson was telling friends he might soon give up business. By now a wealthy man, he seemed to carry on in a consultant role more out of habit and for pleasure than for profit. In fact, although he was no longer taking charge of lines, he was to wield a strong influence on the railways for years to come.

One reason for his continued involvement was his friendship with George Hudson, a schemer whom he first met by chance in 1834. Hudson was so impressed with Stephenson's railway vision that he invested in railways himself, promoting his home town of York as a vital link in the lines north. Initially, Hudson gained credibility by linking his name to Stephenson's projects, but his fame accrued during the 'railway mania' of 1840 to 1845, when every town in the country wanted to build a line. The inclusion of Hudson's name on a prospectus seemed to guarantee success, but in fact his growing wealth and influence were largely due to decidedly dodgy dealings that would soon be illegal under company law – in particular, paying dividends out of new investments. Coupling glitz and bravado with a fine sense of public relations, Hudson was feted in the press, and by 1843 was being dubbed the 'Railway King'. Flattered to have played an integral part in this success story, Stephenson was canny enough to stay on the sidelines, and, when the bubble burst, was not enmeshed in Hudson's downfall. This came in 1848 after independent auditing showed up a trail of embezzlement covered by false accounting.

Hoping to build Hudson's railway going north to Berwick, Stephenson was goaded by an alternative proposal to be engineered by Brunel. Apart from the resentment of a south-

erner on his turf, two issues rankled: Brunel's advocacy of the broad gauge, and his suggestion of using the 'atmospheric' system. Briefly, this involved rejecting locomotives in favour of a set of fixed engines which pumped air out of a continuous tube along the track, with the train being driven by a piston connected via a slit in the tube. Stephenson viewed this system with disdain, regarding it as a reversion to the

Right: Bronze statue of George Stephenson with model of Locomotion *at Chesterfield station.*

Below right: Bench from Chesterfield station bench (National Railway Museum, York).

primitive days of rope haulage. He need not have worried, for, after a big investment in South Devon, it was shown to be unworkable. In fact, neither issue was a problem: Brunel never came north, as it was Hudson's route that was favoured by a government bill.

George Stephenson's main objection to the broad gauge seems to be that it wasn't his. The merits or otherwise of the system were not the issue; despite Brunel's reputation as a visionary, he had failed to see that, as the railway network expanded and lines merged, there had to be a single system. To settle the issue, in 1846, Brunel and Robert Stephenson arranged trials on stretches of line from Paddington to Didcot and from Darlington to York. The broad gauge was a clear winner for speed, comfort and reliability, but a government commission ruled that all new railways must be built to Stephenson's 'standard' gauge, with even the Great Western having gradually to change its track width.

Meanwhile, in 1843, George Stephenson moved to another country mansion, but he was still not ready for retirement. Working on a line from Chesterfield, he sensed another business opportunity and bought land near Clay Cross, coupling coal mining and limestone quarrying with an ironworks. Tapton House was to remain his home. When he was not growing prize vegetables in his garden and hothouses, he could show off to his friends on the railway running below his grounds, which became his personal plaything. George Stephenson died in 1848 and is buried at the end of the line in Holy Trinity, Chesterfield.

ROBERT STEPHENSON, THE COMPLETE ENGINEER

By the 1830s, the Stephensons' policy of both specifying and supplying locomotives for their lines unchallenged was superseded by a tender process: possible conflict of interest forced Robert to be less involved with locomotive development and manufacture. With *Patentee*, their first design to be protected by patent, manufacture was offered under licence to other works. The ongoing success of their own locomotives can be measured by their use on non-Stephenson lines: *John Bull*, supplied to the Camden & Amboy Railroad (two ferry rides short of Philadelphia to New York), is now on display in Washington's Smithsonian Institution, and a reproduction *North Star*, the first locomotive for the Great Western, is on view in the Steam Museum at Swindon.

By 1840, if Robert had just sat back in his office chair, despite his huge contribution to steam locomotion, he might be remembered only as the son of the famous George. However, more great achievements were ahead of him in the field of civil engineering, most notably his big bridges. As he moved on to take a more overall role, there were two projects in which he was deeply involved – the Newcastle & Berwick and the Chester & Holyhead lines. The line to Scotland would be marked by Stephenson's crossings of the Wear, the Tyne and the Tweed – all splendid structures with the High Level Newcastle Bridge being particularly celebrated.

The Chester & Holyhead was to be the scene of both a setback and of Stephenson's greatest success. The bridge over the Dee at Chester was a composite of cast and wrought iron, a larger version of a type much used. But the design of the bridge came under close scrutiny when it collapsed with a train on it soon after its completion in 1846, with the loss of five lives. At the inquest, Stephenson, persuaded by the company, maintained that the disaster had been caused by the train being derailed and hitting a girder. This may not have been true. Professional solidarity ensured that every eminent engineer (even Brunel and Locke, who both avoided cast iron in railway bridges) rallied to Stephenson's support, and despite talk of a manslaughter charge, he emerged only shocked and shaken.

Setting aside the disaster, to the west lay Stephenson's greatest challenge and his greatest triumph: the Britannia Bridge over the Menai Straits. Telford had caused a sensation with his suspension bridge, but this possibility would seem to be ruled out. Stephenson had seen the effect a train had had on Captain Brown's suspension bridge at Stockton: 'The undula-

Below: Arnside Viaduct.

Above: Original masonry pier, Britannia Bridge.

Right: Working the replica Planet *class at Liverpool Road (Manchester Museum of Science and Industry).*

tions into which the roadway was thrown … were such as to threaten the instant downfall of the whole structure.' Stephenson came up with a solution even more innovative than Telford's: in conjunction with shipbuilder William Fairburn, he fabricated a square-section wrought iron tube big enough for a train to run through. The initial thinking was that the tube's strength would need to be bolstered by suspension (the tube itself being stiff enough to avoid the 'Captain Brown' oscillations). However, advice and experimentation showed that the two huge spans required could be self-supporting. This great concept was given a smaller-scale trial back along the line at Conwy, and it was there that the extraordinary untried method of floating the thousand-ton tubes on rafts to lift them into position was proved.

So to Menai: Stephenson's team had satisfied themselves in principle at Conwy, but the massive task in the treacherous waters of the Straits was on a different scale. This time the tubes would have to be raised 100 feet, not 20, and the wind and the tide would cause havoc. In 1850, heroic acts of engineering were enjoyed by the public almost as a sporting contest – their authors regarded as film stars or footballers today. As at Rainhill, vast crowds gathered to watch the 'performance', but the spectators on the Anglesey shore could not have anticipated how they were about to be involved. As the pontoon loaded with the first tube was being manoeuvred into position a 12-inch cable jammed in its winch, which was then ripped from its foundation. The foreman, in an extraordinary act of bravery,

grabbed the cable, freed it from the winch and, shouting to the crowd to help, manhandled it up the shore. Joining in what must have been the most desperate tug-of-war ever, these bystanders hauled the raft and its 1500-ton tube back into line to dock it into position and save the day.

After the death of his wife in 1842, Stephenson led a lonely life, and by the late 1850s he was not a strong or well man, having overworked himself for two decades. Acting as a consultant for foreign schemes helped him reduce day-by-day management pressures; as well as more 'tube' bridges for lines in Egypt and Canada, he was involved with railways in Italy and Norway. One of the pleasures of his later years was sailing an ocean yacht – at sea he felt free of all business pressures. It was on one such trip to

Norway in 1859 that he was taken ill, and, despite a rushed voyage home over the North Sea, he died soon after, aged only 56. Just a month earlier, his friend Brunel, equally worn out by work, had died at the even younger age of 53.

Robert Stephenson had become a national figure. He was an MP, president of both the Civil Engineers and the Mechanical Engineers institutions and (unlike his father) carried his success with a most appealing modesty. He was mourned in an unprecedented way: from the Thames to the Tyne, ships stopped their business and flew flags at half-mast; with the Queen's permission, the funeral procession travelled through Hyde Park to Westminster Abbey, where he was buried in the nave of Westminster Abbey – the only other engineer to join Thomas Telford there.

Left: Penmaenmawr, on the Holyhead line.

Early Days

Replica of Locomotion *at the National Railway Museum, York
(on loan from Pockerley Waggonway, Beamish)*

Facing page: George Stephenson was born in 1781 in Street House, Wylam in Northumberland. It might sound grand, but the family occupied only one of the four rooms. The track in front of the house, today a cycle route, was a wagonway carrying coal from Wylam Colliery to the Tyne.

Right: The blue plaque on the Boathouse Inn at Newburn commemorates local associations: George Stephenson was married in the village church and worked at Water Row pit, Newburn.

George brought up his son Robert in a cottage at Killingworth; the sundial they made together (below right) shows how Robert's education was supplemented by practical mechanics passed down from father to son. As well as attending private school in the city, Robert was enrolled as a member of Newcastle Literary and Philosophical Society (right) and brought home books to read with his father.

Facing page: In the colliery workshops behind Sundial Cottage, George constructed early locomotives for the Killingworth and Hetton tramways. On display at the National Railway Museum, Shildon, is the earliest surviving Stephenson engine, dated 1822, from the Hetton line.

George Stephenson and Sir Humphry Davy worked separately on the development of a mine safety lamp. Although Davy won the competition, Stephenson later received money raised by subscription on Tyneside and was presented with a silver tankard, shown (right) by Fenella Philpot, archivist at the Institution of Mechanical Engineers.

Below right: Lamps by Davy and Stephenson are on display in the Royal Institution of Great Britain, London.

Facing page: Professor Frank James shows an early Stephenson lamp (on the table) and one by Davy, in the lecture theatre of the Royal Institution, where Davy conducted his research.

The historic 1821 meeting between George Stephenson and Edward Pease took place at the latter's Darlington house, 73 Northgate (far right).

The principal purpose of the Stockton & Darlington is well illustrated by the trackside remains at Shildon (facing page and below right). Prominent are the impressive goods shed and the drop walls, where coal in colliery trams was tipped into the wagons.

A ruined stable (right) underlines the fact that passenger trains were to be horse-drawn.

NZ215255

The ironwork (right) is in the National Railway Museum, York, and is a section of the Gaunless viaduct, the first iron railway bridge.

At Brusselton, the pattern of stonework on the cottage wall (below right) is a reminder of the old engine house. Just to the west, an original bridge (below left) has been by-passed by a breach in the embankment.

Facing page: Stone bearers allowed the horses to walk down the middle of the track, without having to step over cross-tie sleepers.

Locomotion

In the early days of the Stockton & Darlington, carriages were pulled by horses, and Pease did not think of using steam until George Stephenson took him to Killingworth to see his engines at work. Pease's new enthusiasm led Stephenson to set up in business at the Forth Street Works.

Locomotion, *seen here on display at the Head of Steam museum, Darlington, was Stephenson's first engine for the Stockton & Darlington. Far right: stoking a replica of* Locomotion *at the National Railway Museum, York.*

Facing page: The engine shed at Pockerley Waggonway, Beamish, contains an original Stockton & Darlington carriage. The structural ironwork is reused from the Forth Street Works.

Right: The grassy slopes of Summerhill Square run up to Greenfield Terrace, where Stephenson lived when he was first married.

Below: Forth Street Works in Newcastle, where Stephenson produced the world's first steam locomotives.

Facing page: The bronze statue of Robert Stephenson in Westgate Street dominates the centre of Newcastle.

(The famous High Level Bridge is featured on pages 94-5.)

Liverpool to Manchester

A replica of Stephenson's Rocket *at the National Railway Museum, York.*

*The original terminus of the
Liverpool & Manchester line was at
Crown Street, today a public park
(facing page). The information
plaque (below right) has been ripped
off its plinth, but a more permanent
memorial is the red brick
tunnel vent.*

*Near the site is Stephenson's house at
Upper Parliament Street (right and
top right.)*

1781 – 1848
GEORGE STEPHENSON

CHIEF ENGINEER
LIVERPOOL & MANCHESTER RAILWAY
LIVED HERE

Facing page: A mile to the west of the Crown Street terminus, Edge Hill was a pivotal point on the line. Carriages freewheeled down from Crown Street, and fixed engines pulled trains up from the docks, and from Olive Mount to the east. The site became a huge goods yard, which today is largely occupied with modern 'shed' businesses. The scale of the operation can be seen from this model in the National Railway Museum, York.

Far right: The original cobbled entrance to the station remains, with the main passenger building (below).

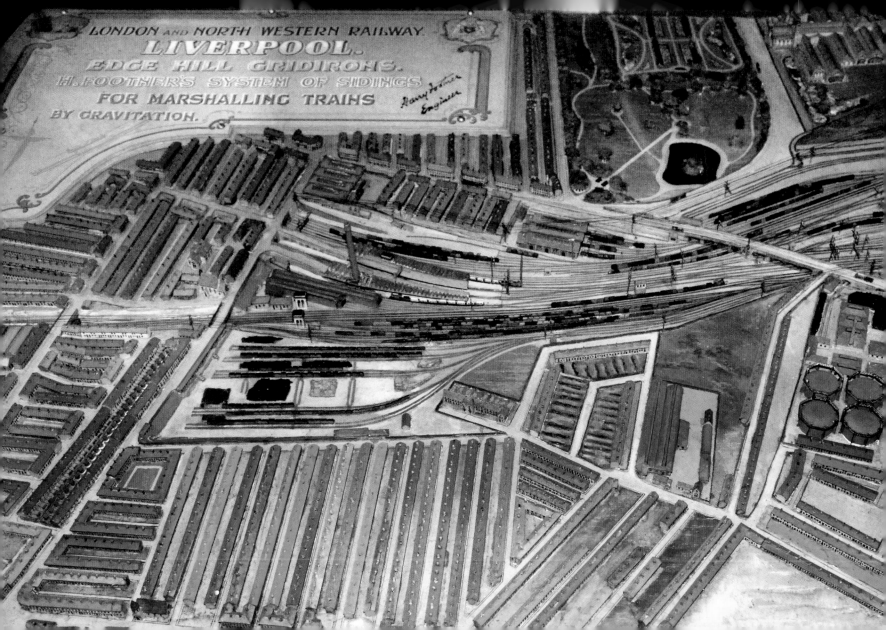

LONDON and NORTH WESTERN RAILWAY.
LIVERPOOL.
EDGE HILL GRIDIRONS.
H. FOOTNER'S SYSTEM OF SIDINGS
FOR MARSHALLING TRAINS
BY GRAVITATION.

Harry Footner
Engineer

Olive Mount

Facing page: At Olive Mount
a deep cut runs through hard rock.

Right: a section of the Edge Hill
winding engine wire rope (National
Railway Museum, York).

RAINHILL

Facing page: The 'skew' bridge at Rainhill station is well known, but Rainhill is most famous for the locomotive trials of 1829, in which Robert Stephenson's newly developed Rocket *triumphed. The replica (right) is at the National Railway Museum, York.*

Rocket *was one of five locomotives to take part in the trials at Rainhill. Timothy Hackworth's* Sans Pareil, *(right, in the National Railway Museum, Shildon) failed in the trials but was later successfully employed on the railway.*

The new features that enabled Rocket *to eclipse the opposition were the steam tubes in the boiler and the lowering of the cylinders to 45 degrees. The original locomotive in the Science Museum (facing page) retains its in-service improvement and has cylinders lowered to be almost horizontal. The model and later replica (far right) faithfully stick to the original design.*

SJ588946

Right: The station at Earlestown, a district of Newton-le-Willows, is reputed to be the oldest in use today. Just to the west, an impressive viaduct crosses the Sankey valley (facing page).

CHAT MOSS

SJ704971
*The biggest challenge on the
Liverpool & Manchester line was to
take the track across an extensive
area of swamp at Chat Moss
(subsequently drained). The feat was
eventually accomplished by building
the embankments on foundations of
willow hurdles!*

The original terminus buildings of the Liverpool & Manchester now form Manchester's Museum of Science and Industry. They include the ticket hall (below right and facing page) and warehouse buildings (right, with the Hilton hotel in the background).

Exhibits at the museum include an original carriage (above right), and a working replica of Planet *(see page 89 – by the time the line opened,* Rocket *had been superseded).*

Consolidation

Snibston Colliery, Coalville.

*Right: Most of the Canterbury &
Whitstable line was worked by fixed
engines, with a small level section
being worked by* Invicta, *an
immediate follow-up to* Rocket.
*The 'driver' provided by Canterbury
Museum illustrates the early literal
meaning of 'footplate'.*

*Facing page: Also on view adjacent
to the museum are remnants from a
winding engine, including a
flywheel (far right).*

SK420156

The main feature of this line was the rope-hauled incline at Swannington (right). The engine (facing page) is in the National Railway Museum, York. Other railway relics can still be seen by the old tracks (below right).

COALVILLE

Tunnelling on the Leicester line revealed coal seams which George Stephenson exploited, buying land and moving to nearby Alton Grange (below) in order to be closer to the work. The lift bridge (facing page) and the remains of the colliery at Snibston (right) are now part of a museum.

George Stephenson's 1839 line from Manchester to Leeds takes the route of the Rochdale Canal across the Pennines between Littleborough and Todmorden. At the village of Summit (below right) it enters a nearly two-mile long tunnel which was the longest in the world when completed, but which was overtaken by Brunel's Box Tunnel a year later.

Facing page: In December 1984, a train of petrol tankers caught fire in the tunnel. Betty Rigg who lives in a cottage just below the line of vents which mark the route through the hill, shows a book with a photo of the resulting inferno. 'The first I knew, a fireman knocked on my door and said "Leave straight away – the whole hillside might blow up!"' It didn't (although the fire took three days to burn out). The tunnel is still in use today.

Right: Over the hill in Gauxholme, a sophisticated skew bridge over the Rochdale Canal provides more unexpected ironwork; the railway deck hangs from a pair of cast iron bows braced by wrought iron tie bars, while the deep steel beams below are 1906 reinforcements.

Facing page: Opposite the Summit tunnel entrance, a handsome aqueduct of iron plates carries the River Roch across the deep approach cutting of the railway.

Completed in 1840, the London to Birmingham was Robert Stephenson's first big project undertaken totally independently of his father. The original terminus at Chalk Farm became the site of a winding engine when the line was extended to Euston, and is today marked by the later locomotive 'roundhouse' (below).

Above: Elegant porticoes around the Primrose Hill tunnel have lost their charm, but emerging from the city, the route borrows the visual attraction of the old Grand Junction Canal. Of its many iron bridges, *none remains as built; the skew bridge at Winkwell (facing page), with its ribs cased in concrete, provides a reminder of the original ironwork.*

SP817508

Softening landscape and a forest of pylons disguise the severity of the cutting north of the station at Tring (right).

Facing page: North of the railway town of Wolverton, a multi-arched brick viaduct crosses the River Ouse.

BLISWORTH

SP753512, 724543

Another deep cutting at Blisworth (right) is followed by a canal crossing (facing page). The Grand Junction provided more than a scenic and ready-made route: as with many railways, the canal was able to facilitate the building of the line, before dying as a result of the new competition from the railways.

Right and facing page:
A handsome viaduct across the
overgrown meadows of the
Warwickshire Avon.

SP569708

Kilsby proved a difficult engineering job, its line today marked by several prominent vent towers (facing page). After the successful completion of the tunnel and the line, the Stephenson clan celebrated in the Dun Cow pub in local Dunchurch (right).

NZ054453, 095490

This line became a rare setback for Robert Stephenson - not in engineering terms, but as a business and financial venture (see page 15). The abandoned winding house of Waskerley (right) stands at the top of 'Nanny Myers' incline (above), but another one marked on the OS map high above Stanhope has now vanished. At Hownes Gill, where Stephenson's original plan used two inclines, a dramatic viaduct spans the ravine (far right and facing page).

CLAY CROSS

As at Leicester, tunnelling revealed coal seams, and soon George Stephenson was on the move again (see page 82). Today there is little to see, but the route of the line under Clay Cross is defined by a series of tunnel vents.

George Stephenson's new financial interest at Clay Cross led him to relocate to his final home, *Tapton House (right)*, a mansion high above Chesterfield, where he spent his spare time watching the trains on the line below and developed a keen interest in horticulture.

Facing page: Chesterfield museum has a collection of Stephenson items, including the old man's patented 'cucumber straightener', shown here by Anne–Marie Knowles, the museum curator.

Robert Stephenson, Complete Engineer

Pedestrians on the High Level Bridge, Newcastle.

Most Victorian engineers spent time working on Fenland drainage at some point in their career. Robert Stephenson was a consultant on the New North Level (facing page), previously improved by Thomas Telford. Structural improvements, as at the Foul Anchor sluice (right), were implemented by his cousin, George Robert Stephenson (see plaque below).

By the time the Liverpool to Manchester line opened, Rocket *had been superseded by developments which led to the* Planet *class.*

Facing page: a replica of Planet *steams at Liverpool Road. In the background is a mural featuring the next progression,* Lion, *of the six-wheeled* Patentee *class.*

Right, above: Lion, *whose history includes a starring role in the 1953 film* The Titfield Thunderbolt, *was built under licence in 1838 by Todd Kitson & Laird of Leeds. Photographed in the Conservation Workshop of National Museums, Liverpool, the engine is to be the centrepiece of the Port City Gallery in the Museum of Liverpool when it opens in 2011. Right below: a replica of* North Star, *a six-wheeled broad gauge locomotive built by Stephenson for the opening of the Great Western (Steam Museum, Swindon).*

Robert Stephenson's next initiative was to lengthen the boiler to enhance the engine's steam-raising ability; this led to the shape of locomotive that would last nearly a hundred years (see page 89).

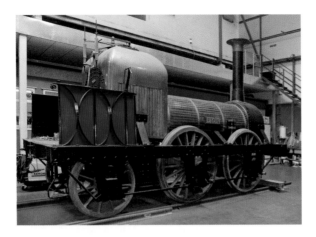

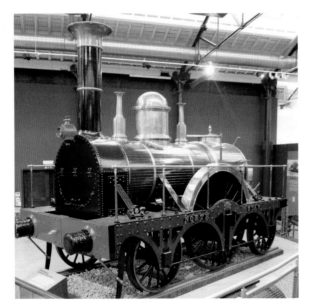

Above: After a merger in 1906, Robert Stephenson & Company built small power station engines such as this saddle tank, dated 1942 (National Railway Museum Shildon). Production finally ceased in 1950.

Gauge Wars

To settle the dispute caused by Brunel's insistence on using the non-standard broad gauge on the Great Western, in 1846, government observers agreed to monitor test runs on the Paddington to Didcot and Darlington to York lines.

Brunel's engine was of the Firefly *class (see modern version, right, Didcot Railway Centre). Robert Stephenson's was an engine featuring his latest long-boiler design, a type similar to the North East Railways 1275 in the National Railway Museum, York (facing page).*

Despite the broad gauge giving by far the best performance, the practical difficulties of nonconformity led the government to rule against the seven-foot system, and no new broad-gauge lines were built.

George Stephenson also fretted about Brunel's other maverick idea - the 'atmospheric' vacuum-driven scheme (Didcot, right). He needn't have worried: it was an immediate failure.

NZ920545

Right and facing page: Victoria Bridge, crossing the River Wear at Penhaw, completed the route from the Thames to the Tyne.

Right and facing page: The High Level Bridge between Gateshead and Newcastle is a splendid cast iron memorial to Britain's finest nineteenth-century engineer. The bridge is double-decked: trains run on the top, with a road and pedestrian routes beneath.

The Royal Border Bridge at Berwick was the final link in the line from London to Edinburgh.

ARNSIDE

On the west coast, the Stephensons worked on a cautious coastal route through Cumbria, unlike the adventurous Joseph Locke, whose successful Glasgow line took the hills at Shap head-on regardless of gradient. Here, Arnside Viaduct takes a low profile across the non-navigable river Kent estuary.

Right: The bridge at Conwy on the Chester to Holyhead line (previous page, with Telford's suspension bridge) is a miniature version of the Britannia Bridge which once spanned the Menai Straits (see page 104.)

Facing page: From Conwy, the Chester to Holyhead line clings to the cliff edge on a sea wall round the Penmaenmawr headland, the sun dipping into the horizon between Anglesey and Puffin Island.

Facing page: Sadly altered following a fire, the Britannia Bridge is Robert Stephenson's most important claim to fame. Consisting of a daring fabricated tube cantilevered between massive stone piers, its original form can be seen in a lithograph at the Institution of Civil Engineers (see page 8). Its square-section tubes (right) have been called the prototype of the modern 'box-girder' system of bridge design.

The replacement, built on top of the original piers, is a double deck with the road on top. The rail tracks running underneath (above) offer an eerie reference to the tubes of the original structure.

A Place in History

The Stephensons were at the height of their powers during the second quarter of the nineteenth century. It seems strange that a father and son could largely share the same period, but George was a late arrival and Robert a precocious youth who died young.

It was the inventiveness of Cornishman Richard Trevithick in modifying the steam engine that led to the possibility of steam locomotion, but Trevithick's prowess was not allied with commercial ability and he died a pauper. Trevithick's ideas were taken up by several mechanics who were running horse-drawn wagonways in the collieries, particularly on Tyneside. All found many obstacles in their way. The one who persevered and who was strong enough to overcome one problem after another, was the stoic George Stephenson. Stephenson's extraordinary mechanical aptitude (which initially won him favour with his colliery-owner bosses), coupled with a canny manipulative ability in winning contracts, thrust him from pit worker to a household name within two decades. By 1840, his name on a railway proposal was a passport to success.

George Stephenson only gained literacy as an adult in night school, and all his life suffered from perceived snubs from scientists and established professionals. The best-documented incidents are the treatment he received from Sir Humphry Davy and the humiliation in parliament over his Liverpool survey. The story that he was refused membership of the Institution of Civil Engineers in 1846 is denied by that body, but it is easy to see how the story persisted. If he had been told to list his qualifications and experience in order to qualify as a member, as required in the rule book, it would have been a red rag to a bull. What is certainly true is that, later the same year, he accepted an invitation to become the first president of the newly formed Institution of Mechanical Engineers, based in Birmingham. According to the 'Mechanicals', the timing was coincidental, but the fragmentation which began that year was to be continued, leaving the engineering profession today represented by a variety of different bodies. With hindsight, it may well have been a turning point, marking the beginning of the end for the heroic Victorian engineer and the start of a steady eclipse of engineering by the architectural profession.

George Stephenson's son Robert inherited his father's mechanical aptitude. Many talented sons follow in their fathers' footsteps and feel stifled. In this case, the father was undoubtedly a controlling man, but Robert was still allowed big responsibilities. A three-year spell in South America must have given him confidence in his own abilities, and he was to show a wider spectrum of talent than his father. As well as his mechanical ability, his proven skills included surveying, parliamentary presentation, business management and

ultimately, planning innovative solutions in iron bridge design. He served as president of the Civil Engineers, as well as following his father in the same role with the 'Mechanicals'.

Two other engineers, direct contemporaries of Robert Stephenson, stand shoulder to shoulder with him. One, Joseph Locke, trained as an apprentice with George Stephenson. When he finally broke away (with much bad grace on Stephenson's part), he became a railway builder of the first rank, taking Telford's views on canals and roads that the straight

Far left: Marble bust of Robert Stephenson in the Institution of Mechanical Engineers, London.

Left: Bronze statue of Robert Stephenson in Euston station, London.

Right: Robert Stephenson's final resting place in Westminster Abbey, London.

Facing page: A stained glass window in Westminster Abbey commemorates the Stephensons' greatest achievements. Depicted are Britannia Bridge , Newcastle High Level Bridge and Rocket.

route was worth fighting (and digging) for, whereas George Stephenson, like Brindley, was happy to follow the contours. When his father died, Robert Stephenson re-established a friendship with Locke. His other competitor – and, it should be emphasised, his very good friend – was Isambard Kingdom Brunel. Also the son of a famous engineer, Brunel was a charismatic extrovert with the ability to sway a committee behind his plans. Rather like George Stephenson, he had a jealously controlling character and could not bear to share responsibility, or even to delegate. His most famous project was the Bristol Railway, a brilliant success due to his choice of route including – against all advice – the two-mile Box Tunnel, which arrived in London soon after Robert Stephenson's Birmingham line. Less successful were his determination to pursue his 'broad gauge' and his fanciful ideas of the 'atmospheric' railway. Determined to be in charge of every aspect of all his projects, Brunel even specified engine design, but he was no mechanical engineer, and the Great Western Railway was only saved by his employing Daniel Gooch – trained in Stephenson's locomotive factory in Newcastle – who developed the best locomotives in the country and went on to become the company's chairman.

When the Britannia tubes were lifted into position at Menai, Brunel was right by Stephenson's side on the pontoons, offering moral and technical support. Robert had never shared his father's antipathy to Brunel, and although Brunel had been a rival in promoting different ways for railway development, he and Robert had been friends since the early 1840s. Stephenson later reciprocated this act of solidarity with support for Brunel's

own big bridge at Saltash and at the difficult launch of the *Great Eastern*. Both Brunel and Robert Stephenson died young, essentially from overwork, within a month of each other. Extraordinarily, within six months the other great railway engineer, their contemporary Joseph Locke, who had been a pallbearer at Stephenson's funeral, was also dead. All three of these great men were in their mid-fifties. Visionaries they may have been, but as boys at the beginning of the century, even they could not have guessed how Trevithick's locomotive, developed and exploited in their hands, would have changed the world for ever.

Index

Note: References to George and Robert Stephenson occur throughout the book and are not included in this index.

Alton Grange 15, 62
Anglesey 20
Arnside 19, 98-9
atmospheric steam engine 17, 90
Berwick 17, 19, 96-7
Billy 3
Blisworth 16, 72-3
Britannia Bridge 8, 19, 104-5
broad gauge 17, 90
Brunel, Isambard Kingdom 17-18, 108-9
Brusselton 32-3

Canterbury 58-9
Cambourne 3
Chat Moss 11, 52-3
Chester 19
Chesterfield 18, 82-3
Clay Cross 80-1
Coalville 15
Conwy 20, 100-2
Crown Street, Liverpool 41

Davy, Sir Humphry 28
Dun Cow 76

Earlestown 50
Edge Hill 42-4
Euston 106

Firefly 90

Forth Street 34-6

Gauxholme 15, 66
Gaunless 32
Grand Junction Canal 68-9, 72-3
Grand Junction Railway 14
Hedley, William 8, 26
High Level Bridge, Newcastle 19, 85, 94-5
Hownes Gill 79
Hudson, George 17
Institution of Civil Engineers 8, 21, 106-7
Institution of Mechanical Engineers 21, 28, 106-7
Invicta 58

James, William 11
Killingworth 8, 10, 26-7
Kilsby 15, 77
Leicester 60-1
Lion 88, 111
Liverpool 40-1
Literary & Philosophical Society of Newcastle Upon Tyne 9, 26
Locke, Joseph 14, 98, 109
Locomotion 10, 23, 34
London & Birmingham 15

Manchester 54-5, 89
Menai 19-20
miner's safety lamp 28
'Nanny Myers' Incline 78
Newburn 24
Newcastle 26, 36-7, 85
Newcomen, Timothy 5, 7
New North Level 86-7
North Star 88

Olive Mount 11, 45

Patentee 88
Pease, Edward 10, 30
Penmaenmawr 103
Penshaw 92-3
Pen-y-Darren 5, 7
Planet 89
plateway 8
Primrose Hill 68
Puffing Billy 1, 23, 26

Rainhill 13, 47
Rocket 13, 39, 46-9
Roundhouse 68
Royal Border Bridge, Berwick 96-7
Royal Institution of Great Britain 28-9

Sankey 11, 51
Sans Pareil 13, 48

Savery, Thomas 5
Shildon 30-1, 35
Snibston 15, 57, 62-3
Stanhope & Tyne 15, 78-9
Stephenson, George Robert 86
Stockton & Darlington 10-11, 30-5
Summit 64-5, 67
Swannington 60-1

Tapton House 82
Telford, Thomas 12, 16
Trevithick, Richard 5, 7, 12
Tring 70

Waskerley 78
Watt, James 5, 7
Westminster Abbey 108-9
Winkwell 69
Wolston 74-5
Wolverton 71
Wylam 8, 25

Lion *detail, National Museums, Liverpool.*

Acknowledgements and Further Reading

The author would like to thank

    Mike Chrimes
    John Clarke
    Anthony Cools
    Sarah and Tim Goffe
    John Liffen
    Carol Morgan
    Paul Sharman
    – and all those who agreed to appear in this book.

Especial thanks to Mark Whitby for his involvement, and to Paul Manning for design and editing.

The book would be far from complete without the co-operation of many institutions and museums:

    Canterbury Museum
    Chesterfield Museum
    Didcot Railway Centre
    Head of Steam, Darlington Railway Museum
    The Institution of Civil Engineers
    The Institution of Mechanical Engineers
    The Manchester Museum of Science & Industry
    The Museum of Liverpool
    Pockerley Waggonway, Beamish Museum
    The Royal Institution of Great Britain
    The Science Museum, London
    Steam Museum, Swindon
    The Stephenson Railway Museum, North Shields
    The National Railway Museum, Shildon
    The National Railway Museum, York
    The North Level Drainage Board
    Westminster Abbey

Further Reading

Bailey, Michael R., ed., *Robert Stephenson: The Eminent Engineer* (Ashgate, 2003)

Davies, Hunter, *George Stephenson: The Remarkable Life Of The Founder Of The Railways* (Sutton, 2004)

Rolt, L.T.C., *George and Robert Stephenson: The Railway Revolution* (Amberley, 2009)

Rosen, William, *The Most Powerful Idea in the World: A Story of Steam, Industry, and Invention* (Random House, 2010)

Ross, David, *George & Robert Stephenson: A Passion For Success* (The History Press, 2010)

Useful Websites

www.engineering-timelines.com
www.erih.net
www.makingthemodernworld.org.uk
www.stephensonloco.org.uk